# ALL ABOUT ME
# KEEPING WELL

Dan Lester and Madeleine Marie

**W**
FRANKLIN WATTS
LONDON • SYDNEY

First published in Great Britain in 2023 by Hodder & Stoughton

Copyright © Hodder & Stoughton Limited, 2023

All rights reserved.

Series Editor: Victoria Brooker
Series Designer: Lisa Peacock

Some of the material in this book first appeared in *Tiger Talk Growing Up* by Leon Read (Franklin Watts).

HB ISBN: 978 1 4451 8658 0
PB ISBN: 978 1 4451 8659 7

Printed in Dubai

Franklin Watts
An imprint of
Hachette Children's Group
Part of Hodder & Stoughton
Carmelite House
50 Victoria Embankment
London EC4Y 0DZ

An Hachette UK Company
www.hachette.co.uk

| London Borough of Enfield |||
|---|---|---|
| 91200000798912 |||
| Askews & Holts | 20-Sep-2023 ||
| J613  JUNIOR NON-FICT |||
| ENWINC |||

# CONTENTS

| | |
|---|---|
| Keeping well | 4 |
| Eat well | 6 |
| Brushing teeth | 8 |
| Good exercise | 10 |
| Washing hands | 12 |
| Feeling ill | 14 |
| Taking medicine | 16 |
| What a mess! | 18 |
| Clean clothes | 20 |
| Bath time! | 22 |
| Time for bed | 24 |
| Keeping safe | 26 |
| Feeling great | 28 |
| Parent and teacher notes | 30 |
| Index | 32 |

# KEEPING WELL

It's important to keep healthy and safe. We can do lots of things to keep well.

Eat healthy food

Drink water

# EAT WELL

We need to eat a well-balanced diet. This includes eating lots of fruits and vegetables a day.

Which foods do you eat?

stew and dumplings

pizza and chips

chicken and rice

pasta

# BRUSHING TEETH

We need to look after our teeth.

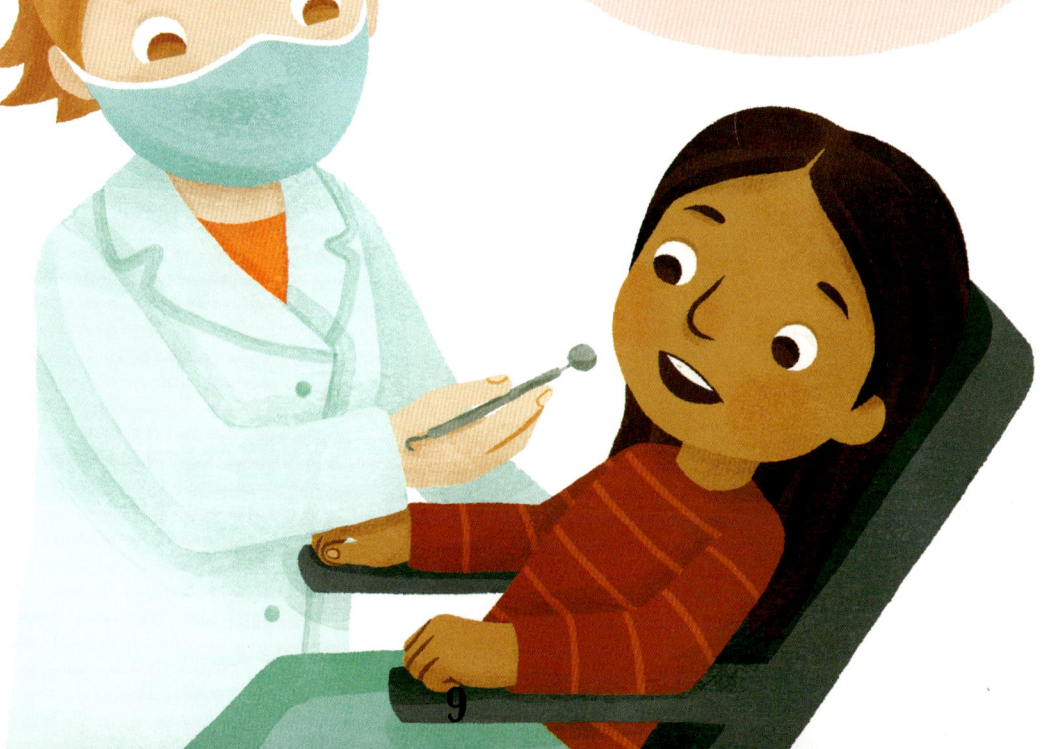

# GOOD EXERCISE

Exercise makes us strong.

We can exercise by

skipping ...

dancing ...

running ...

or stretching.

What is your favourite exercise?

# WASHING HANDS

Before we eat we wash our hands to get rid of dirt and germs.

Wash your hands after going to the toilet and before you eat.

Use warm water and soap. Rub your hands together to make foam. Then rinse with water.

# FEELING ILL

Germs can make us ill. Germs are tiny. We can only see them using a machine.

I'm drawing a picture of a germ.

Germs can give us colds, coughs, fevers or sickness.

The best way to avoid getting ill is to keep clean.

When was the last time you visited the doctor?

# TAKING MEDICINE

Sometimes we need medicine to make us better.

Only adults are allowed to give medicine.

Medicine must be given in the right amount otherwise it can make you more ill.

# WHAT A MESS!

Help to keep things clean and tidy. Germs like mess.

I help my dad clean up.

Untidy mess can cause accidents.

Look out! Lucy has tripped over.

Why should Lucy tidy her bedroom?

# CLEAN CLOTHES

Clothes get dirty too! Put on clean underwear and socks every day.

Sports clothes can get extra smelly and dirty.

# BATH TIME!

Imagine what would happen if you did not wash.

You would smell!

It's important to keep clean.

And having a bath is fun, too!

# TIME FOR BED

Everyone needs sleep. Without sleep we get tired and ill.

I like sleeping and dreaming.

What do you dream about when you sleep?

What time do you go to bed?

# KEEPING SAFE

To keep safe, listen to adults you trust and follow their advice.

Wear a helmet when riding a bike.

Wear suncream on a hot, sunny day.

If a stranger tries to talk to you, walk away and tell an adult.

Never go near water without an adult.

# FEELING GREAT

There are lots of different things we can do to keep well.

Adam is in a muddle.
Help him remember how to keep well.

What do I need to do before I eat food?

Why do I need to sleep?

Why do I need to exercise?

Why do I need to tidy my bedroom?

# PARENT AND TEACHER NOTES

Teaching notes and activities by Maureen Gallagher, educational consultant and author. These notes and activities will help you make the most of this book with your child or class.

COMMUNICATION, LANGUAGE AND LITERACY

SPEAKING AND LISTENING
- Look at the front cover – what does the child think the book will be about? What does the child on the front cover need to do with his hands?
- What does the child know about how to stay fit and well?
- Look at the contents list. Talk about what the child likes to eat. What are their favourite foods? How many fruit and vegetables can the child name, how many have they eaten?
- Look at the section on 'Good Exercise'. What other types of exercise can the child think of – what other exercise do they do? Do they walk or scooter to school, what games do they play at break times, what do they do in the park, what exercise could they do at home?
- Look at the section on 'Feeling ill'. Has the child ever felt ill and had to visit the doctor? How did the doctor help them; did they have to take any medicine? Talk about the importance of only taking medicine which is prescribed for you.

READING
- Ask the child to read to you. Are there any particular letters and sounds the child has difficulty with? If so, remind them of their sounds.
- If the child is only just starting to learn to read, then read the book to the child and enjoy it together. Point out the words 'can' 'we' and 'you' and encourage the child to read them whenever they appear.
- Encourage the child to look closely at the pictures and talk about what they can see. Do they make the text clearer? Do they help the child to work out what some words are?
- Encourage the child to look closely at the pictures. Do they help the child to work out what some words are?
- Talk about the difference between fiction and non-fiction books. Explain how the contents list works and ask the child to use it to find you the section on washing hands. Can they work out what section they will find a picture of a toothbrush in? Where might they find a picture of a sleeping child? Check and see if they are right.

## WRITING

- Can the child draw and label a list of things to do to stay healthy?
- Does the child have a favourite letter of the alphabet? Can they write it? Can they write their name? What other letters can they write? Make a poster of the letters of the alphabet together that the child can display somewhere.
- Encourage them to make a sign with their name on to put on their bedroom door or on one of their possessions. Make it colourful and bright.
- Can the child remember any of their dreams? If so, draw a picture of something that happened and write a sentence below to explain. If they can't remember, ask them to draw an exciting event with them in it, and write a sentence describing what is happening.

## PERSONAL, SOCIAL AND EMOTIONAL DEVELOPMENT

- Ask the child why the following things are important and what happens if they don't have enough of them: sleep, healthy food, clean hands and body, exercise.

## PHYSICAL DEVELOPMENT

Talk about all the physical changes that have happened to the child since birth and all the things they can do now like walking, running, jumping, climbing, hopping, skipping, throwing and catching – can they show you how well they can do each of these things?

## PROBLEM SOLVING, REASONING AND NUMERACY

- Can the child work out how much sleep they have every night? Show them how to tell the hour on an analogue clock. What time do they go to bed at and when do they get up in the morning?
- How many times a day do they wash their hands? How often do they brush their teeth?

## UNDERSTANDING OF THE WORLD

- Talk about water. How many different things does the child use it for? Where does it come from? Talk about why it is important not to waste water and explain that some people in the world don't have running water in their homes but have to walk to a tap or a well to fetch it just as people did in this country in previous centuries. Ask the child to imagine what life would be like if they had to fetch all the water they use from a well some distance away. Would it change how much water they use?

# INDEX

clean 5, 12, 13, 15, 18, 20, 23

exercise 5, 10, 11

food 4, 6, 7

germs 12, 14, 15 18

illness 15, 16, 17

medicine 17, 17

safety 26, 27
sleep 24, 25

teeth 8, 9

water 4